Light and Easy
PASTA

The endless possibilities and convenience of pasta and noodles have been appreciated the world over for centuries. The Chinese, Germans and even the French – and, of course, the Italians – all feature different forms of pasta in their national cuisines. Simple, speedy, versatile, economical, nutritious and always delicious, pasta is sure to please every time. Now you can learn how to cook your pasta to perfection – and even how to make your own – from the recipes in this collection. Pasta is cooked when it is tender but still retains a 'bite'. The term for this is al dente. *Fresh pasta cooks very quickly, often requiring only a minute or two, and is ready when it rises to the surface of the boiling water. Dried pasta takes longer; as a general guide, allow 8-12 minutes, but test frequently. Drain the pasta as soon as it is cooked and place it in a heated dish to which a little butter or oil has been added. Whether you're in search of traditional favourites or new combinations, soups, starters, salads or main meals, you'll find them here.*

CONTENTS

FRESH PASTA AND EASY SAUCES

*There's nothing quite like the joys of creating your own pasta –
and children just love it! A pasta machine is convenient but not
necessary. In fact some claim handmade is so much the better!*

Basic Pasta Dough

250g (8oz) plain flour
2 eggs
1 tspn olive oil
pinch salt

To make pasta by hand

Sift flour into a mound on a flat surface. Make a well in the centre and add eggs, oil and salt. Blend egg mixture into flour, first with a fork, then with your hand, gradually working in enough of the flour to make a soft dough. Scrape down and clean work surface and dust lightly with flour. Knead dough for 8-10 minutes or until soft, smooth and elastic.

To make pasta by food processor

Place 185g (6oz) flour and salt in a food processor fitted with plastic blade. With motor running, add eggs and oil and process, pulsing machine on and off, for 2 minutes or until dough is soft, smooth and elastic. Add a little water or more flour as needed to adjust consistency.

Coloured Pasta: To make green pasta, add 2-3 tablespoons very dry, finely chopped cooked spinach with eggs and oil; for red pasta, add 1-2 tablespoons tomato purée with eggs and oil.

To roll pasta by machine

1 Set rollers at maximum width. Cut dough into four pieces. Flatten one piece and run it through rollers. Fold piece into thirds, give it a quarter turn and run it through rollers again. Repeat procedure three more times or until dough feels smooth and elastic and has a satin glow. Repeat procedure with remaining pieces.

2 Reduce width between rollers one notch and run dough pieces, one at a time, through rollers again. Lay sheets on a cloth as you work. Continue reducing width of rollers, one notch at a time, until dough is flattened to desired thickness. Cut into strips using appropriate cutter and spread pasta out on tea-towels to dry.

To roll pasta by hand

Allow dough to rest, covered, for 30 minutes. Roll out dough on a lightly floured surface as you would pastry into a large thin sheet, giving the dough a quarter turn every few rolls. Cut and shape as desired. The pasta can be cooked straight away or dried and stored as for commercial pasta.

Basic Shapes

Ribbon noodles: Cut dough sheets into 25-30cm (10-12in) wide strips. Loosely roll each strip over on itself three or four times. Using a very sharp knife cut roll crosswise into strips: 3mm (1/8in) for tagliolini, 5mm (1/4in) for tagliatelle, 1cm (1/2in) for fettucine and 2cm (3/4in) for pappardelle. Unravel and spread noodles out on a clean tea-towel to dry or hang over a towel on a rack or a piece of dowling or a broom handle set horizontally.

Lasagne: Cut dough sheets into 12cm (5in) squares. When cooking, add pieces, one at a time, to boiling water to which 1 teaspoon oil has been added to prevent sticking. Cook for 2-3 minutes.

Cannelloni: Follow instructions for lasagne, then place a spoonful of your chosen filling in centre of each square of cooked pasta. Roll up into tubes, arrange in a buttered ovenproof dish and top with sauces of your choice.

Makes 250g (8oz) pasta to serve 4-6

Kitchen Tip

Pasta cooking times vary. Freshly made pasta cooks in 2-3 minutes. Purchased fresh pasta cooks in 4-6 minutes and dried commercial pasta in 6-10 minutes – or more if the pasta is thicker.

Frying pan & bowls Accoutrement

Quick Meat Sauce, Pesto (page 4)

Quick Meat Sauce

15g (¹/₂oz) butter

375g (12oz) lean minced beef

2 fresh thin spicy Italian sausages, casings removed

1 small bay leaf

¹/₂ onion

1 whole clove

2 tomatoes, chopped

beef stock, wine or water

salt

1 Melt butter in a heavy frying pan and add beef, sausage mince, bay leaf and onion studded with clove. Cook over low heat, stirring frequently and breaking up lumps, for 20 minutes or until meat is well browned.

2 Add tomatoes and bring to the boil. Reduce heat and simmer gently, adding a little stock, wine or water if sauce becomes too dry, for 45-50 minutes. Season with salt to taste and remove onion and bay leaf before serving.

Serves 4-6

Fettucine with Garlic Butter

375g (12oz) fettucine

90g (3oz) butter

2 cloves garlic, slivered

125g (4oz) freshly grated Parmesan cheese

1 Cook fettucine in boiling salted water until *al dente*. Drain and set aside, reserving a little of the cooking liquid.

2 Melt butter in a large saucepan over low heat, add garlic and cook without browning for 1 minute. Add fettucine to pan and toss well. Add Parmesan cheese and toss again, adding reserved cooking liquid if pasta is too dry. Serve immediately.

Serves 2-4

Pesto

2-3 cloves garlic, chopped

4-6 tblspn finely chopped fresh basil

4 tblspn chopped fresh parsley

1 tblspn pine nuts

60g (2oz) freshly grated Parmesan or Romano cheese

250ml (8fl oz) olive oil

freshly ground black pepper

1 With a mortar and pestle, pound garlic, basil, parsley, pine nuts and Parmesan or Romano cheese together until smooth. Alternatively, place in a blender or food processor and process until smooth.

2 Add oil gradually, whisking or processing well between additions, until sauce is thick and smooth. Season to taste with black pepper. If making large quantities, place in a jar, cover with a layer of olive oil, seal and store in the refrigerator.

Makes 375g (12oz)

Kitchen Tip
Pesto is a Genoese sauce used with all kinds of pasta and gnocchi. Try a tablespoon stirred into minestrone or chicken broth at the last minute, or a spoonful with baked potatoes, or add pesto to taste to vinaigrette salad dressings – delicious over tomatoes and fresh fennel.

Pasta with Herb Cream Sauce

45g (1¹/₂oz) butter

250ml (8fl oz) double cream

2 tspn grated lemon rind

1 tblspn lemon juice

3 tblspn chopped mixed fresh herbs such as chervil, chives, dill, oregano, sage, parsley

freshly ground black pepper

250g (8oz) fettucine

1 Melt butter in a saucepan and stir in cream, lemon rind, lemon juice and herbs. Bring slowly to the boil, reduce heat and simmer, stirring constantly, until cream reduces by one-third. Remove from heat, season to taste with black pepper and set aside.

2 Cook fettucine in boiling salted water until *al dente*. Drain thoroughly and return to pan over low heat. Add cream sauce, toss well and serve immediately.

Serves 4-6

Light Tomato Sauce

1 tblspn olive oil

1 clove garlic, crushed

2 spring onions, chopped

4 tomatoes, peeled, seeded and chopped

2 tspn tomato purée

freshly ground black pepper

15g (¹/₂oz) butter

Heat oil in a saucepan over low heat, add garlic and spring onions and cook for 2-3 minutes. Add tomatoes and tomato purée and season to taste with black pepper. Cook, stirring occasionally, for 10 minutes or until sauce thickens. If you prefer a smooth sauce, purée in a blender or food processor. Just prior to serving, stir in butter.

Serves 4

Kitchen Tip
This light, fresh-tasting sauce is very versatile. Serve it with noodles or your favourite pasta, roast beef, or grilled meats or chicken. Add a handful of chopped fresh parsley for colour and vitamin C.

Linguine with Walnut Sauce

Linguine with Walnut Sauce

90g (3oz) walnuts, toasted

2 cloves garlic

15g (1/2oz) butter

freshly ground black pepper

1 tblspn olive oil

60ml (2fl oz) double cream

1 tblspn freshly grated Parmesan cheese

3 tblspn chopped fresh basil

1 tblspn lemon juice

250g (8oz) dried or fresh linguine

freshly grated Parmesan cheese, extra to serve

1 Place walnuts, garlic, butter and black pepper to taste in a blender or food processor and process until smooth. With motor running, gradually add oil, blending until well combined. Add cream, Parmesan cheese, basil and lemon juice and process for a few seconds or until just combined.

2 Cook linguine in boiling salted water until *al dente*. Drain well, reserving 250ml (8fl oz) cooking liquid. Return pasta to pan and set aside. Add half the reserved cooking liquid to walnut sauce, mixing until smooth and creamy, adding more liquid only if necessary.

3 Pour sauce over pasta and toss well to combine. Transfer to a warmed dish and serve immediately, sprinkled with extra Parmesan cheese.

Serves 4

Kitchen Tip
Linguine looks like spaghetti, but with square-cut ends. The walnut sauce is also good with spaghetti, fettucine or tagliatelle.

Party Entrées and Light Lunches

These fabulous recipes are sure to kick off your dinner to a stylish start and leave you plenty of time to enjoy yourself – and the compliments!

Linguine 'Pizzaiolo'

375g (12oz) linguine

90g (3oz) freshly grated Parmesan cheese

Pizzaiolo Sauce

3 tblspn olive oil

3 firm, ripe tomatoes, peeled, seeded and roughly chopped

2 cloves garlic, crushed

2 tspn chopped fresh basil or oregano

1 tspn Dijon mustard

2 tblspn chopped fresh parsley

freshly ground black pepper

1 Cook linguine in boiling salted water until *al dente*. Drain and set aside to keep warm.

2 To make sauce, heat oil in a saucepan over low heat, add tomatoes and garlic and cook for 5 minutes. Add basil or oregano and mustard to pan and cook for 2 minutes longer. Stir in parsley and black pepper to taste and remove from heat. Spoon sauce over pasta and sprinkle with Parmesan cheese.

Serves 4

Kitchen Tip
This simple Neapolitan sauce, made with good, fresh red tomatoes (canned will do in an emergency) should retain its fresh taste and look if you avoid overcooking.

Straw and Grass with Caviar

125g (4oz) ribbon pasta such as tagliolini, tagliatelle, fettucine, pappardelle

125g (4oz) spinach ribbon pasta

90g (3oz) butter

1 clove garlic, chopped

200g (6½oz) red salmon caviar or red lumpfish roe

lemon wedges to serve

1 Cook pastas separately in boiling salted water until *al dente*. Drain and return to one pan, add butter and garlic and toss well.

2 Arrange pasta on heated serving plates. Top with caviar and a lemon wedge. Squeeze lemon over pasta before eating.

Serves 4

Kitchen Tip
A fascinating name – the two coloured noodles represent the straw and grass. Look for large golden-red eggs of Canadian salmon at good supermarkets or delicatessens – if not available, use pressed red lumpfish roe.

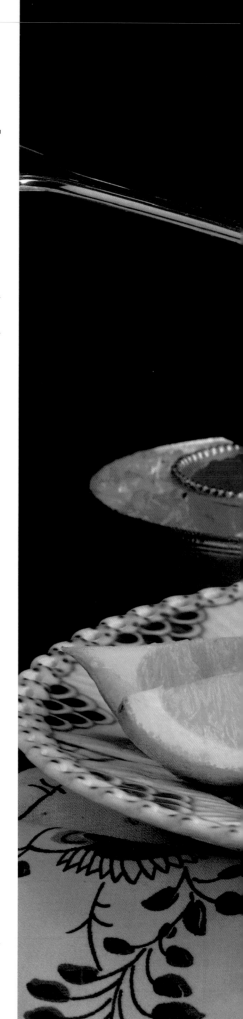

Straw and Grass with Caviar

Tortellini Gorgonzola

375ml (12fl oz) dry white wine

500ml (16fl oz) double cream, scalded

freshly ground black pepper

freshly grated nutmeg

750g (1½lb) tortellini

250g (8oz) gorgonzola cheese (not over-ripe), crumbled

1 tblspn freshly grated Parmesan cheese

1 Place wine in a saucepan, bring to the boil and boil until reduced by half. Add heated cream, bring slowly to the boil, reduce heat and gently simmer for 15 minutes or until mixture reduces and thickens slightly. Season to taste with black pepper and nutmeg.

2 Cook tortellini in boiling salted water until *al dente*. Drain and return to pan over low heat. Stir half the gorgonzola cheese into cream mixture, add Parmesan cheese and pour over tortellini.

3 Toss pasta with sauce until cheese is melted. Spoon onto heated plates and sprinkle with remaining gorgonzola. Serve immediately.

Serves 6

Bucatini 'Ammuddicata'

4-5 canned anchovy fillets

milk

170ml (5½fl oz) olive oil

90g (3oz) coarse breadcrumbs, made from stale bread

pinch chilli powder

250g (8oz) bucatini

2-3 tblspn chopped fresh parsley, optional

1 tspn chopped fresh oregano, optional

1 Soak anchovies in a little milk for 15-20 minutes, drain and chop. In a small saucepan, heat half the oil over very low heat, add anchovies and cook, stirring, until dissolved to a paste.

2 Heat remaining oil in a frying pan over moderate heat, add breadcrumbs and stir fry until crisp. Sprinkle with chilli powder, transfer to a bowl and set aside to keep warm.

3 Cook bucatini in boiling salted water until *al dente*. Drain well and toss with anchovy sauce, and parsley and oregano (if using). Sprinkle with breadcrumbs and serve immediately.

Serves 3-4

Kitchen Tip
Bucatini are fine noodles with a tiny hole running through them. This quick, easy, delicious dish is from southern Italy and traditionally, no cheese is served with it.

Macaroni with Mascarpone

280g (9oz) elbow macaroni

3 egg yolks, at room temperature

6 tblspn grated Parmesan cheese

125g (4oz) mascarpone

freshly ground black pepper

freshly grated nutmeg

1 Cook macaroni in boiling salted water until *al dente*. Drain and set aside to keep warm.

2 Place egg yolks and Parmesan cheese in a heated bowl placed over a saucepan of simmering water and mix to combine. Add mascarpone, black pepper and nutmeg to taste and mix well. Add very hot macaroni, toss well and serve immediately.

Serves 4

Kitchen Tip
Use a large soup tureen or heatproof serving bowl to prepare this dish. Keep the container hot by placing it over a saucepan of simmering water as you add and mix the ingredients so that the egg yolks cook in the sauce.

Tortellini Gorgonzola

Tagliatelle, Spinach and Prosciutto

Tagliatelle, Spinach and Prosciutto

250ml (8fl oz) double cream

60g (2oz) grated Parmesan cheese

freshly ground black pepper

500g (1lb) spinach, stems removed, washed and dried

1 tblspn olive oil

4 slices prosciutto or ham, cut into thin strips

375g (12oz) tagliatelle

Parmesan cheese shavings for garnish

1 Place cream in a small saucepan and stir in grated Parmesan cheese. Cook over moderate heat, stirring constantly, for 3-5 minutes or until cheese melts. Season to taste with black pepper and set aside to keep warm.

2 Steam or microwave spinach until wilted. Heat oil in a small frying pan, add prosciutto and cook over moderate heat until hot.

3 Cook pasta in boiling salted water until *al dente.* Drain well and divide between serving plates. Top with spinach leaves and prosciutto, then carefully pour sauce over. Garnish with Parmesan shavings and serve.

Serves 4

Spaghetti with Goats' Cheese

1 x quantity Light Tomato Sauce, see recipe page 4

100g (3¹/₂oz) goats' cheese, cut into chunks

Tabasco sauce

375g (12oz) spaghetti

1 Prepare tomato sauce following recipe directions, then add goats' cheese and stir until cheese softens. Season to taste with Tabasco sauce; it should be a little fiery.

2 Cook spaghetti in boiling salted water until *al dente.* Drain well and return to pan. Add sauce, toss through and serve immediately.

Serves 4

Smoked Salmon Fettucine

280g (9oz) fettucine

30g (1oz) butter

185ml (6fl oz) double cream

125g (4oz) smoked salmon, cut into slivers

ground white pepper

1/2 tspn snipped fresh chives

1 tblspn caviar or black lumpfish roe for garnish, optional

1 Cook fettucine in boiling salted water until *al dente*. Drain well and set aside to keep warm.

2 Melt butter in a large frying pan over moderate heat, add cream and cook for 2-3 minutes or until mixture reduces slightly. Add salmon and heat for 3 minutes.

3 Add fettucine to mixture, increase heat and cook, tossing well, for 2 minutes. Sprinkle with white pepper to taste. Serve garnished with chives and caviar or lumpfish roe (if using).

Serves 4

Penne with Clams

375g (12oz) clams or pipis, scrubbed or 200g (6 1/2 oz) canned clams

6 tblspn olive oil

90g (3oz) shelled fresh or frozen peas

280g (9oz) penne

1 tblspn chopped fresh parsley

freshly ground black pepper

1 If using fresh clams or pipis, soak in cold water for 2 hours to disgorge sand. Drain and place in a large frying pan over high heat, cover and heat for 2-3 minutes or until shells open. Discard any unopened shells. Remove remaining clams from shells and set aside. Strain and reserve pan liquid. If using canned clams, drain and reserve liquid.

2 Place 125ml (4fl oz) reserved clam liquid and oil in a frying pan. Add peas, bring to the boil, reduce heat and simmer for 12 minutes (4 minutes if using frozen peas). Add clams and cook for 2 minutes more.

3 Cook penne in boiling salted water until *al dente*. Drain well, add to clam mixture with parsley and black pepper to taste. Heat through, stirring, for 1 minute before serving.

Serves 4

Fusilli with Mussels

500g (1lb) mussels, scrubbed and beards removed

250g (8oz) potatoes, diced

100ml (3 1/2 fl oz) olive oil

250g (8oz) fusilli

2 tblspn chopped fresh parsley

freshly ground black pepper

1 Soak mussels in cold water for 2 hours to disgorge sand. Drain well and place in a large frying pan over high heat. Cover and heat for 5 minutes or until shells open. Discard any unopened shells. Remove mussels from remaining shells and set aside. Strain and reserve pan liquid.

2 Boil, steam or microwave potatoes until just tender and drain. Heat oil in a frying pan over moderate heat, add mussels and potatoes and cook, stirring, for 2 minutes. Add 6 tablespoons reserved liquid and stir to combine.

3 Cook fusilli in boiling salted water until *al dente*. Drain well and add to frying pan with parsley and black pepper to taste. Stir for 1 minute before serving.

Serves 4

Left: Smoked Salmon Fettucine
Right: Penne with Clams

SALADS AND LIGHT MAIN MEALS

Pasta can be as hearty or as simple as you like. These easy and speedy salad suggestions are no less exotic and could take centre stage at your summer table.

Curried Pasta and Chicken Salad

250g (8oz) fusilli

2 boneless chicken breast fillets, poached

6 cherry tomatoes, halved

3 spring onions, thinly sliced

1 tblspn finely chopped fresh basil

Curry Dressing

1 tblspn butter

1 clove garlic

1 tspn grated fresh ginger

1 tspn curry paste

pinch cayenne pepper

60ml (2fl oz) double cream

1 tblspn white vinegar

1 tblspn finely chopped mango chutney

freshly ground black pepper

1 Cook pasta in boiling salted water until *al dente*. Drain, refresh under cold water and drain again.

2 Cut chicken into chunks and place in a bowl. Add pasta, tomatoes, spring onions and basil and lightly toss to combine.

3 To make dressing, melt butter in a saucepan over low heat, add garlic, ginger, curry paste and cayenne pepper and gently cook, stirring, until onions are soft. Add cream and bring to the boil, whisking until mixture slightly thickens. Whisk in vinegar and chutney.

4 Pour dressing over pasta mixture, season to taste with black pepper and toss well. Serve at room temperature.

Serves 6

Pork Teriyaki Pasta

1 x quantity Basic Pasta Dough, see recipe page 2

1/2 tspn freshly ground black pepper

Teriyaki Cream Sauce

250g (8oz) pork leg steak, trimmed and pounded thinly

1 tblspn olive oil

30g (1oz) butter

20 small mangetout, strings removed

1 tspn teriyaki sauce

250ml (8fl oz) double cream

1 Prepare basic dough following recipe directions, adding pepper to egg mixture before mixing into the flour. Roll dough and cut into fettucine ribbons.

2 To make sauce, cut pork into small medallions or strips. Heat oil and butter in a frying pan over moderately-high heat, add pork and stir fry for 4-5 minutes or until golden and almost cooked. Add mangetout and stir fry for 1 minute more. Add teriyaki sauce and cream to pork and simmer until sauce bubbles and slightly thickens.

3 Cook pasta in boiling salted water to which a little oil has been added for 3-4 minutes or until *al dente*. Drain well and transfer to warm serving plates. Spoon pork mixture with sauce over pasta and serve.

Serves 4

Pork Teriyaki Pasta

Tortellini Artichoke Salad

500g (1lb) fresh or frozen tortellini

2 large red peppers, thinly sliced

6-8 sun-dried tomatoes in oil, drained and cut into strips

410g (13oz) canned artichoke hearts (plain or marinated), drained and quartered

2 spring onions, diagonally sliced

3 tblspn fresh basil leaves

1 tblspn lemon juice

1 tspn Dijon mustard

2 tspn balsamic vinegar or malt vinegar

60ml (2fl oz) vegetable oil

60ml (2fl oz) light olive oil

freshly ground black pepper

1 Cook tortellini in boiling salted water following packet directions until *al dente*. Drain well and place in a large mixing bowl.

2 Blanch red peppers in boiling water for 1-2 minutes, drain and refresh under cold water and drain again. Add to tortellini with tomatoes, artichokes and spring onions and lightly toss to combine.

3 Place basil, lemon juice, mustard and vinegar in a blender or food processor and process for 1 minute. With motor running, gradually add oils in a thin, steady stream and process until thick. Season to taste with black pepper.

4 Pour dressing over salad and toss well. Transfer mixture to a serving bowl and serve at room temperature.

Serves 6

Fettucine Vegetable Salad

375g (12oz) fettucine

1 tblspn olive oil

3 courgettes or 6 baby squash, cut into 1cm (1/2in) slices

125g (4oz) green beans or asparagus, cut into 2.5cm (1in) lengths

60g (2oz) mangetout, strings removed, optional

2 tblspn chopped mixed fresh herbs, such as parsley, oregano, basil

Garlic Lemon Dressing

4 tblspn olive oil

1 clove garlic, finely chopped

2 tblspn lemon juice

1 tblspn vinegar

freshly ground black pepper

1 Break fettucine into shorter lengths and cook in boiling salted water until *al dente*. Drain and refresh under cold water. Drain again and toss with 1 tablespoon oil in a large bowl.

2 Blanch vegetables separately in boiling salted water, just long enough to set colours and retain crunch. Drain and refresh under cold water. Drain again and add to pasta.

3 To make dressing, place 4 tablespoons oil, garlic, lemon juice, vinegar and black pepper to taste in a screwtop jar and shake well to combine. Pour over pasta mixture, sprinkle with herbs and toss well. Serve at room temperature.

Serves 6

Spaghetti 'alla Puttanesca'

60ml (2fl oz) olive oil

2 cloves garlic, 1 crushed, 1 finely chopped

3 tomatoes, peeled and chopped

8 black olives, pitted

1/2 hot fresh red chilli, or Tabasco sauce to taste

1 tblspn capers

1 tspn chopped fresh oregano

freshly ground black pepper

4 anchovy fillets, chopped

2 tblspn chopped fresh parsley

375g (12oz) spaghetti or linguine

1 Heat oil in a saucepan over moderate heat, add crushed garlic and cook until brown. With slotted spoon, remove and discard garlic.

2 Add chopped garlic, tomatoes, olives, red chilli or Tabasco sauce, capers, oregano and black pepper to taste to pan. Cook, stirring, over moderately-high heat for 12-15 minutes or until sauce thickens. Add anchovies and parsley and cook for 2 minutes longer. Remove chilli.

3 Cook pasta in boiling salted water following packet directions until *al dente*. Drain well and place on serving plates. Top with sauce and serve immediately.

Serves 4

Red Pepper and Ricotta Pasta

250g (8oz) spaghetti or tagliatelle

250g (8oz) ricotta cheese

3 canned red peppers, drained and chopped

1 clove garlic, chopped

1-2 tblspn lemon juice

freshly ground black pepper

2 tblspn freshly grated Parmesan cheese

2 tspn finely grated lemon rind

3 tblspn chopped fresh herbs, such as parsley, thyme, oregano, chives

1 Break pasta into 20cm (8in) lengths and cook in boiling salted water until *al dente*. Drain and refresh under cold water and drain again.

2 Place ricotta cheese in a large bowl and beat with a wooden spoon until smooth. Add red peppers, garlic and lemon juice, season to taste with black pepper and mix well.

3 Add pasta to ricotta mixture and toss well. Sprinke with Parmesan cheese, lemon rind and herbs and serve at room temperature.

Serves 4

Pasta Salad with Smoked Eel

Pasta Salad with Smoked Eel

250g (8oz) penne

250-315g (8-10oz) smoked eel or smoked trout

8 sun-dried tomatoes in oil, halved, if large

12-16 small black olives

1 small red onion, sliced

salad greens, prepared and crisped

1 lemon, cut into wedges for garnish

Mustard Chutney Dressing

2 tspn Dijon mustard

6 tblspn virgin olive oil

2 tspn balsamic vinegar

1 tblspn mayonnaise

1 tblspn fruit chutney

1 Cook penne in boiling salted water until *al dente*. Drain and refresh under cold water, drain again and place in a bowl.

2 To make dressing, place mustard in a small bowl and gradually add oil, whisking until mixture thickens. Whisk in vinegar, then mayonnaise and chutney. Toss through pasta and set aside to marinate for 30 minutes.

3 Remove skin from eel or trout, remove fillets from backbone and slice. Add to pasta mixture with tomatoes, olives and onion and lightly mix.

4 To assemble salad, line dinner plates with salad greens, top with pasta mixture and garnish with lemon wedges.

Serves 4

Pasta and Broccoli Salad

750g (1¹/₂lb) broccoli, cut into small florets

1 red pepper, very thinly sliced or shredded

250g (8oz) pasta spirals or shells

1 tblspn chopped fresh parsley

Garlic Dressing

1 egg

2 cloves garlic, crushed

freshly ground black pepper

60ml (2fl oz) olive oil

60ml (2fl oz) vegetable oil

2 tblspn white wine vinegar

1 Steam broccoli or blanch in boiling water for 4 minutes or until just tender, adding red pepper to broccoli for the last minute to lightly blanch. Drain vegetables, refresh under cold water, drain again and place in a large bowl.

2 Cook pasta in boiling salted water until *al dente*. Drain, refresh under cold water, drain again and add to vegetables.

3 To make dressing, place egg, garlic and black pepper to taste in a blender or food processor. Add 1 tablespoon olive oil and process for 20-30 seconds. With motor running, gradually add remaining oils and process until dressing thickens. Add vinegar and mix to combine.

4 Add dressing to pasta mixture, sprinkle with parsley and toss until combined. Serve at room temperature.

Serves 6-8

Pasta and Salami Salad

250g (8oz) large shell macaroni

3 tblspn olive oil

2 cloves garlic, crushed

30g (1oz) pine nuts

100g (3¹/₂oz) salami, sliced

1 tblspn chopped fresh parsley

1 Cook macaroni in boiling salted water following packet directions until *al dente*. Drain.

2 Heat oil in a large frying pan over moderate heat. Add garlic and pine nuts and cook, stirring constantly, for 1 minute or until pine nuts are golden. Remove pan from heat, stir in salami, parsley and pasta and serve.

Serves 4

Linguine with Olive Clam Sauce

375g (12oz) linguine or spaghetti

45g (1¹/₂oz) canned anchovy fillets, drained and roughly chopped

250g (8oz) canned clams, drained

75g (2¹/₂oz) pitted black olives, chopped

2 cloves garlic, chopped

1-2 tblspn lemon juice

freshly ground black pepper

90ml (3fl oz) olive oil

4-5 tblspn chopped fresh parsley

1 Cook linguine in boiling salted water following packet directions until *al dente*. Drain and refresh under cold water and drain again. Set aside to thoroughly drain.

2 Place anchovies, clams, olives, garlic, lemon juice and black pepper to taste in a large bowl and mix to combine. Gradually add oil, whisking until mixture slightly thickens.

3 Add pasta to anchovy mixture and toss to coat. Sprinkle with parsley and serve at room temperature.

Serves 4

Spaghetti Caruso

4 tblspn olive oil

2 cloves garlic, halved

2 medium onions, chopped

250g (8oz) chicken livers, cleaned and chopped

250g (8oz) button mushrooms, sliced

2 tblspn tomato purée

125ml (4fl oz) water

440g (14oz) chopped canned tomatoes in juice, undrained

1 tspn each chopped fresh thyme and basil or ¹/₄ tspn each dried thyme and basil

1 bay leaf

1 tspn sugar

freshly ground black pepper

500g (1lb) spaghetti or bucatini

125g (4oz) freshly grated Parmesan cheese

1 Heat 3 tablespoons oil in a saucepan over moderate heat, add garlic and cook for 2 minutes and discard. Add onions to pan and cook, stirring, for 4 minutes. Add chicken livers and mushrooms and cook, stirring constantly, for 5 minutes or until livers are brown. Remove pan from heat.

2 Place tomato purée, water, tomatoes and their juice, herbs, sugar and black pepper to taste in a small bowl and mix well to combine. Stir into liver mixture and bring to the boil. Reduce heat and simmer, covered, for 30 minutes.

3 Cook spaghetti in boiling salted water with remaining oil following packet directions until *al dente*. Drain well, place on a heated serving platter and sprinkle with half the Parmesan cheese. Spoon over half the sauce and toss lightly to combine. At the table, offer remaining sauce and cheese separately.

Serves 4-6

Chicken and Tortellini Pesto Salad

500g (1lb) tortellini

1 x quantity Pesto, see recipe page 4

410g (13oz) boneless chicken breast fillets, poached and cut into slivers

1 small onion, thinly sliced

4 tblspn chopped fresh parsley

4 tblspn snipped fresh chives

200g (6¹/₂oz) natural yogurt

2-3 tspn olive oil, optional

freshly ground black pepper

1 Prepare Pesto following recipe directions. Cook tortellini in boiling salted water following packet directions until *al dente*. Drain, refresh under cold water, drain again and place in a large bowl. Add Pesto, toss well and set aside to marinate 2 hours at room temperature.

2 Add chicken and onion to tortellini mixture with 3 tablespoons each of the parsley and chives and lightly mix. Add yogurt and mix well. Stir in a little oil if the salad seems dry, season to taste with black pepper and serve with remaining herbs.

Serves 6-8

Curry Cream Pasta and Salmon

250g (8oz) fusilli

250g (8oz) asparagus or green beans, trimmed

185g (6oz) sour cream

2 tblspn lemon juice

1-2 cloves garlic, chopped

1¹/₂ tspn curry powder or curry paste

freshly ground black pepper

125g (4oz) smoked salmon, cut into julienne strips

1 small onion, grated

1 tblspn drained capers

flat-leaved parsley for garnish, optional

1 Cook pasta in boiling salted water following packet directions until *al dente*. Drain and refresh under cold water and drain again.

2 Boil, steam or microwave asparagus until just tender. Drain, cut into 2.5cm (1in) pieces and set aside.

3 Place sour cream, lemon juice, garlic, curry powder and black pepper to taste in a large bowl and mix to combine. Stir in salmon, onion and capers.

4 Add pasta and asparagus to curry mixture and toss lightly. Garnish with parsley (if using) and serve immediately.

Serves 4

Kitchen Tip
You can buy smoked salmon offcuts which are economical and excellent for this recipe. If you prefer other seafoods, try smoked mussels or canned crab meat.

Spaghetti with Red Clam Sauce

3 tblspn olive oil

2 cloves garlic, crushed

3 tomatoes, peeled, seeded and chopped

1 tblspn tomato purée

280g (9oz) canned clams, drained

freshly ground black pepper

250g (8oz) spaghetti or linguine

2 tblspn chopped fresh parsley

1 Heat oil in a saucepan over moderate heat, add garlic and cook for 30 seconds. Add tomatoes and tomato purée, reduce heat and simmer for 20 minutes or until sauce thickens. Remove from heat, add clams and black pepper to taste and set aside to keep warm.

2 Cook pasta in boiling salted water following packet directions until *al dente*. Drain and return to pan. Pour sauce over pasta, toss well and sprinkle with parsley. Serve with grated Parmesan cheese, if liked.

Serves 3-4

Pasta Primavera

400g (13oz) fettucine

60g (2oz) frozen peas, blanched

1 red pepper, cut into thin strips and blanched

2 courgettes, cut into thin strips and blanched

90g (3oz) peeled pumpkin, diced and blanched

1 tblspn olive oil

¹/₄ tspn freshly ground black pepper

3 tomatoes, chopped

1 tblspn chopped fresh basil

2 cloves garlic, crushed

2 tblspn tomato purée

4 tblspn freshly grated Parmesan cheese

1 Cook fettucine in boiling salted water following packet directions until *al dente*; drain and return to saucepan.

2 Add peas, red pepper, courgettes, pumpkin, oil and black pepper to pasta, toss well and set aside to keep warm.

3 Place tomatoes, basil, garlic and tomato purée in a blender or food processor and process until smooth. Sieve mixture into a small saucepan and bring to simmering.

4 Divide pasta between heated serving plates. Spoon sauce over pasta, sprinkle with Parmesan cheese and serve immediately.

Serves 4

Pasta Primavera

Mexican Pasta Salad

375g (12oz) pasta shells or bows

1 ripe avocado, peeled and cut into large pieces

2 tblspn lime or lemon juice

125ml (4fl oz) hot chicken stock

125g (4oz) sour cream

1/2 onion, roughly chopped

1/2 tspn ground cumin, or to taste

Tabasco sauce

2 canned jalapeño peppers, chopped or 2 fresh red or green chillies

diced tomato, green pepper and fresh coriander leaves for garnish

1 Cook pasta in boiling salted water following packet directions until *al dente.* Drain, refresh under cold water and drain again.

2 Place avocado and lime or lemon juice in a large bowl and mash with a fork until mixture is smooth. Add stock, sour cream, onion, cumin and Tabasco sauce to taste and mix to combine.

3 Add jalapeño peppers or chillies and pasta to mixture and toss until coated. Garnish with tomato, green pepper and coriander. Serve at room temperature.

Serves 4-6

Kitchen Tip
Jalapeño peppers are medium-to-dark chillies that taper to a blunt end and are 5-7.5cm (2-3in) long and 2-2.5cm (3/4-1in) wide. They are medium-to-hot in taste.

Linguine with Mushrooms and Ham

60g (2oz) unsalted butter

250g (8oz) button mushrooms, thinly sliced

6 spring onions, finely chopped

185ml (6fl oz) double cream

315g (10oz) linguine or thin spaghetti

3 slices ham or 6 slices prosciutto, cut into ribbons

60g (2oz) freshly grated Parmesan cheese

freshly ground black pepper

1 Melt butter in a frying pan over moderate heat, add mushrooms and spring onions and cook, stirring, for 2 minutes. Add cream, bring to the boil and simmer until sauce reduces by half.

2 Cook linguine in boiling salted water following packet directions until *al dente*. Drain well and divide between heated serving plates.

3 Add ham or prosciutto to sauce and heat through gently. Stir in Parmesan cheese and black pepper to taste. Top linguine with sauce and serve immediately.

Serves 2-4

Pine Nut and Poppy Seed Pasta

250g (8oz) ribbon noodles, such as tagliolini, tagliatelle, fettucine, papardelle

30g (1oz) butter

60g (2oz) pine nuts

2 tblspn poppy seeds

1 tblspn paprika

1 Cook pasta in boiling salted water following packet directions until *al dente*. Drain and rinse under running water, then drain again.

2 Melt butter in a large frying pan over moderate heat, add pine nuts and fry until golden. Add poppy seeds and paprika and cook, stirring constantly, for 2 minutes longer.

3 Remove pan from heat, add pasta and lightly toss to combine. Serve immediately.

Serves 4-6

Kitchen Tip
Serve as a light dish on its own or as an accompaniment to chicken, veal or steak.

Pasta with Lemon and Egg Sauce

250g (8oz) rice-shaped pasta (orzo)

410g (13oz) canned artichoke hearts (plain or marinated), drained and halved

75g (2¹/₂oz) pitted black olives, halved

125g (4oz) feta cheese, crumbled

snipped fresh dill for garnish

Dilled Lemon Sauce

2 large egg yolks

2 tblspn lemon juice

2 tspn Dijon mustard

6 spring onions, chopped

3 tblspn snipped fresh dill

freshly ground black pepper

125ml (4fl oz) hot chicken stock

60ml (2fl oz) olive oil

1 Cook pasta in boiling salted water following packet directions until *al dente*. Drain and rinse under cold water and drain again.

2 To make sauce, place egg yolks, lemon juice, mustard, spring onions, dill and black pepper to taste in a blender or food processor and process until smooth. With motor running, gradually add stock, then oil and process until mixture thickens.

3 Place pasta and sauce in a large bowl, add artichokes, olives and feta cheese and lightly toss to combine. Adjust seasonings, garnish with dill and serve at room temperature.

Serves 4-6

Spaghetti with Calamari

125ml (4fl oz) olive oil

¹/₂ small onion, thinly sliced

350g (11oz) small calamari rings

1 large ripe tomato, peeled, seeded and chopped

1 sprig fresh rosemary

280g (9oz) spaghetti or linguine

freshly ground black pepper

fresh parsley sprigs for garnish

1 Heat half the oil in a frying pan over moderate heat, add onion and fry for 3-4 minutes until transparent. Add calamari to pan and cook for 3 minutes. Add tomato and rosemary and cook, stirring, for 8 minutes longer.

2 Using a slotted spoon, remove calamari from pan and set aside to keep warm. Sieve tomato sauce and return to frying pan. Add remaining oil and calamari and cook for 2 minutes longer.

3 Cook spaghetti in boiling salted water following packet directions until *al dente*. Drain well and add to sauce. Add black pepper to taste and toss well to combine. Serve immediately garnished with parsley.

Serves 4

Fusilli, Goats' Cheese and Peppers

1 red pepper, halved and seeded

1 green pepper, halved and seeded

250g (8oz) fusilli

60g (2oz) goats' cheese

500g (1lb) rocket or spinach, well-washed and shredded

8 black olives, pitted and quartered

Mustard Vinaigrette

1 tblspn Dijon mustard

2 tblspn wine vinegar

1 clove garlic, crushed

freshly ground black pepper

6 tblspn olive oil

Fusilli, Goats' Cheese and Peppers

1 Place red and green peppers under a preheated hot grill and cook until skins blacken and blister. Seal peppers in a paper bag and set aside until cool enough to handle. Peel off and discard skins and cut flesh into long strips.

2 To make vinaigrette, place mustard in a large bowl, add vinegar, garlic and black pepper to taste and whisk to combine. Gradually add oil, whisking until dressing thickens.

3 Cook pasta in boiling salted water following packet directions until *al dente*. Drain well, add to vinaigrette and toss to combine. Crumble goats' cheese over pasta mixture, add red and green peppers, rocket or spinach and olives and toss well to combine. Cover and refrigerate for at least 1 hour before serving.

Serves 6

Italian Pasta Salad

315g (10oz) macaroni, such as elbows, shells, bows, spirals
2 tblspn olive oil
250g (8oz) thickly sliced leg ham, cubed
125-250g (4-8oz) black olives, pitted and halved
125g (4oz) fresh shelled or frozen peas, cooked and drained
125-250g (4-8oz) mayonnaise
2 tblspn French mustard
freshly ground black pepper
2 tomatoes, quartered for garnish

1 Cook macaroni in boiling salted water with half the oil following packet directions until *al dente*. Drain, rinse under cold water and drain again. Place pasta in a bowl with remaining oil, ham, olives and peas and toss well.

2 Combine half the mayonnaise with mustard, add to pasta and toss lightly, adding enough of the remaining mayonnaise to make mixture creamy. Season to taste with black pepper. Garnish with tomatoes and chill before serving.

Serves 4-6

FAMILY FAVOURITES

No matter what shape, size or flavour you prefer, everybody loves a plate of pasta. This selection of classic requests is sure to include everyone's favourites.

Bows with Mushrooms and Peas

250g (8oz) pasta bows

2 tblspn olive oil

6 spring onions, chopped

125g (4oz) button mushrooms, sliced

125g (4oz) shelled fresh or frozen peas

1 tspn sugar

2 tblspn chicken stock or water

freshly ground black pepper

6 thin slices prosciutto or ham, shredded

1 Cook pasta in boiling salted water following packet directions until *al dente.* Drain, return to pan and set aside to keep warm.

2 Heat oil in a saucepan over moderate heat, add spring onions and mushrooms and cook, stirring, for 3 minutes. Add peas, sugar, stock or water to pan, season to taste with black pepper and bring to the boil. Reduce heat and simmer briskly for 5 minutes (2 minutes if using frozen peas).

3 Add prosciutto to peas and cook gently for 3 minutes. Pour sauce over pasta, toss well and serve.

Serves 4

Fettucine, Ham and Pepper Salad

250g (8oz) fettucine

1/2 x quantity Mustard Vinaigrette, see recipe page 20

2 yellow, red or green peppers, halved

2 thick slices smoked ham, cubed

90g (3oz) Gruyère cheese, cubed

6-8 black olives

1 Cook fettucine in boiling salted water following packet directions until *al dente.* Drain well and set aside. Prepare vinaigrette following recipe directions.

2 Place red and green peppers under a preheated hot grill and cook until skins blacken and blister. Seal peppers in a paper bag and set aside until cool enough to handle. Peel off and discard skins and cut flesh into long strips.

3 Place peppers, ham, Gruyère cheese and olives in a salad bowl. Add vinaigrette and pasta and mix lightly to combine. Cover and chill for at least 1 hour before serving.

Serves 6

*Bows with Mushrooms and Peas
Fettucine, Ham and Pepper Salad*

'Ragu alla Bolognese'

1 tblspn olive oil
250g (8oz) lean minced beef
250g (8oz) lean minced pork
60g (2oz) bacon or prosciutto, chopped
1 clove garlic, peeled
1 onion, finely chopped
2 tblspn chopped fresh parsley
1 bay leaf
440g (14oz) chopped canned tomatoes in juice, undrained
125ml (4fl oz) white wine
125ml (4fl oz) water
2 tblspn tomato purée
freshly ground black pepper
1 tblspn chopped fresh basil or oregano
butter or double cream, optional

1 Heat oil in a large saucepan over moderate heat. Add beef, pork, bacon or prosciutto, garlic, onion, parsley and bay leaf and cook, stirring frequently to break up lumps, until meat is brown. Discard garlic.

2 Add tomatoes and their juice to pan with wine, water, tomato purée and black pepper to taste and stir to combine. Bring to the boil, reduce heat, cover and gently simmer for 1 hour. Add herb and cook for 1 minute longer. Remove from heat and add a little butter or a few spoonfuls of cream (if using).

Makes enough for 500g (1lb) pasta

Kitchen Tip
Ragu is the sauce from Bologna on which people all over the world have based Bolognaise Sauce. The true ragu however is not that simple; ingredients include several kinds of meat, chicken livers and good uncured bacon, or better still, prosciutto. Sometimes a small cup of double cream or a good piece of butter is added to the sauce just before it is tossed with the hot pasta to give a creamier texture.

Penne Salami Carbonara

375g (12oz) penne
4 eggs, lightly beaten
3 tblspn double cream
30g (1oz) freshly grated Parmesan or Romano cheese
1/2 tspn salt
freshly ground black pepper
90g (3oz) butter
250g (8oz) salami in one piece, diced
2 tblspn snipped fresh chives or finely chopped fresh parsley

1 Cook pasta in boiling salted water following packet directions until *al dente*. Drain well.

2 Place eggs, cream, Parmesan cheese, salt and black pepper to taste in a bowl and mix to combine.

3 Melt butter in a heavy-based frying pan over moderate heat, add salami and cook until light brown. Add egg mixture to pan and cook, stirring, until eggs are just beginning to thicken. (Take care eggs do not begin to scramble). Add pasta and chives or parsley and toss to coat.

Serves 4

Tomato Sauce

2 tblspn olive oil
2 rashers bacon, diced
1 onion, chopped
1 tblspn plain flour
1kg (2lb) fresh tomatoes, peeled and chopped or 2 x 440g (14oz) chopped canned tomatoes in juice, undrained
1 tblspn tomato purée
1 fresh thyme sprig or 1/4 tspn dried thyme
1 bay leaf
2 tspn brown sugar
1 tspn salt
1/4 tspn freshly ground black pepper

1 Heat oil in a heavy saucepan over moderate heat, add bacon and onion and cook, stirring, until onion is golden. Blend in flour.

2 Add tomatoes with juice, tomato purée, herbs and sugar and bring to the boil, stirring. Season with salt and black pepper and simmer, stirring occasionally, for 45 minutes or until sauce thickens.

Makes enough for 500g (1lb) pasta

Tortellini with Peperoni

500g (1lb) tortellini
125g (4oz) peperoni sausage, thinly sliced
4 tomatoes, peeled and seeded
1 tblspn Dijon mustard
1 clove garlic, chopped
2 tspn lemon juice
1 tspn dried red pepper flakes
125ml (4fl oz) olive oil
6 spring onions, finely chopped
basil leaves for garnish

1 Cook tortellini in boiling salted water following packet directions until *al dente*. Drain and refresh under cold water and drain again.

2 Reserve a few slices peperoni for garnish. Place remaining peperoni, tomatoes, mustard, garlic, lemon juice and red pepper flakes in a blender or food processor and process until roughly chopped. With motor running, gradually add oil and process until well combined.

3 Place spring onions and tortellini in a large bowl. Add sauce and toss to combine. Garnish with basil and reserved peperoni and serve at room temperature.

Serves 4-6

Macaroni Vegetable Soup

Macaroni Vegetable Soup

1.5 litres (2¹/₂pt) chicken stock

1¹/₂ tblspn tomato purée

2 carrots, chopped

1 onion, chopped

1 small green pepper, chopped

2 tspn canned green peppercorns, crushed

1 tblspn chopped fresh basil

125g (4oz) small macaroni, such as elbows, tubes, spirals, rice shapes

freshly grated Parmesan cheese to serve

1 Place stock and tomato purée in a large saucepan and bring to the boil. Add carrots, onion, green pepper, peppercorns and basil and simmer for 10 minutes.

2 Add macaroni and cook for 10 minutes or until macaroni is *al dente*. Serve with Parmesan cheese.

Serves 6

Chick Pea Soup

410g (13oz) chick peas, drained

1.5 litres (2¹/₂pt) chicken or beef stock

4 tblspn olive oil

2-3 slices pancetta or streaky bacon, chopped

2 cloves garlic, chopped

4 tblspn chopped fresh parsley

freshly ground black pepper

200g (6oz) ditalini or other small pasta shapes for soup

freshly grated Parmesan cheese to serve

1 Place chick peas and stock in a large saucepan and bring to the boil. Reduce heat and simmer for 5 minutes. With a slotted spoon, remove half the chick peas, purée in a blender or food processor with a little of the stock. Return purée to saucepan.

2 Heat oil in a separate pan over moderate heat, add pancetta or bacon, garlic and parsley and cook until mixture is golden brown. Add mixture (known as the soffrito) to chick peas, bring to the boil and season to taste with black pepper.

3 Add pasta to soup and cook until *al dente*. The soup will thicken considerably during last stage of cooking. Serve with Parmesan cheese.

Serves 6

Vermicelli Napolitana

60ml (2fl oz) olive oil

45g (1¹/₂oz) butter

¹/₂ onion, finely chopped

750g (1¹/₂lb) ripe tomatoes, peeled, seeded and chopped

freshly ground black pepper

500g (1lb) vermicelli

1 tblspn chopped fresh basil or oregano or 1 tspn dried basil or oregano

125g (4oz) freshly grated Parmesan cheese

1 Heat oil and 15g (¹/₂oz) butter in a heavy saucepan over moderate heat, add onion and cook until softened. Add tomatoes, season to taste with black pepper and simmer, uncovered, for 10 minutes.

2 Cook vermicelli in boiling salted water following packet directions until *al dente*. Drain well and place in a shallow serving dish. Dot with remaining butter and sprinkle with herb and 2 tablespoons Parmesan cheese. Pour sauce over pasta and toss gently to combine. Serve with remaining Parmesan cheese.

Serves 4-6

Curried Cheese Noodle Bake

125g (4oz) wide ribbon pasta

1 egg, beaten

170ml (5¹/2fl oz) double cream

125g (4oz) ricotta or creamed cottage cheese

60g (2oz) raisins

1 tspn curry powder

¹/2 tspn salt

45g (1¹/2oz) breadcrumbs, made from stale bread

30g (1oz) butter, melted

2 tblspn freshly grated Parmesan cheese

1 Preheat oven to 180°C (350°F/ Gas 4). Cook pasta in boiling salted water following packet directions until *al dente*. Drain well.

2 Place egg and cream in a large bowl, mix to combine, then stir in ricotta or cottage cheese, raisins, curry powder and salt. Add hot pasta to mixture and toss well to combine. Transfer mixture to a greased ovenproof dish.

3 Place breadcrumbs and melted butter in a bowl, mix well and sprinkle over pasta mixture. Top with Parmesan cheese. Bake for 20 minutes, then place under a preheated hot grill until topping is golden.

Serves 4

Fettucine Cheese Bake

375g (12oz) plain or spinach fettucine

250g (8oz) cottage or ricotta cheese

185g (6oz) sour cream

1 clove garlic, crushed

2 onions, finely chopped

3 canned red peppers, drained and chopped

¹/4 tspn salt

1 tspn Worcestershire sauce

dash Tabasco sauce

90g (3oz) grated Cheddar, Gouda or Edam cheese

1 Preheat oven to 180°C (350°F/ Gas 4). Cook fettucine in boiling salted water following packet directions until *al dente*. Drain, rinse in hot water and drain again.

2 Place fettucine in a large bowl, add cottage or ricotta cheese, sour cream, garlic, onions, red peppers, salt, Worcestershire sauce and Tabasco sauce to taste and mix well.

3 Transfer mixture to a greased 1.2-1.5 litre (2-2¹/2pt) oven-proof dish, sprinkle with grated cheese and bake for 20 minutes or until bubbly and golden.

Serves 4

Lasagne

500g (1lb) lasagne sheets

500g (1lb) ricotta cheese

500g (1lb) mozzarella cheese, thinly sliced

125g (4oz) freshly grated Parmesan cheese

Tomato Meat Sauce

60ml (2fl oz) olive oil

1 large onion, finely chopped

1 clove garlic, crushed

2 tblspn chopped fresh parsley

250g (8oz) lean minced beef

250g (8oz) lean minced pork

2 x 440g (14oz) chopped canned tomatoes in juice, undrained

2 tblspn tomato purée

1 tblspn chopped fresh basil or 2 tspn dried basil

1 tblspn sugar

1 tspn salt

1 tspn dried oregano leaves

¹/4 tspn freshly ground black pepper

1 To make sauce, heat oil in a heavy saucepan over moderate heat, add onion, garlic and parsley and cook, stirring, for 5 minutes or until onion is tender. Add beef and pork and cook, stirring to break up lumps, until well browned.

2 Add tomatoes with juice, tomato purée, basil, sugar, salt, oregano and black pepper to mixture. Bring to the boil, reduce heat, cover and gently simmer, stirring occasionally, for 2 hours or until sauce thickens.

3 Preheat oven to 180°C (350°F/ Gas 4). Cook lasagne, 2-3 sheets at a time, in boiling salted water with a splash of olive oil for 8-10 minutes or until *al dente*. Drain, rinse under hot water and drain again.

4 Spoon a little sauce into a greased 32 x 23cm (12³/4 x 9 in) ovenproof dish. Top with a layer of lasagne sheets, then ricotta cheese, mozzarella cheese, sauce and Parmesan cheese. Repeat layers until all ingredients are used, ending with sauce and Parmesan.

5 Bake, uncovered, for 45-50 minutes or until cheese is melted and top is golden brown. Remove and set aside to stand for 10-15 minutes before cutting.

Serves 8-10

Chicken Pasta Bake

250g (8oz) pasta of your choice

¹/2 cooked chicken, skin and bones removed, flesh roughly chopped

6 spring onions, chopped

1 red pepper, chopped

350g (11oz) canned pineapple pieces, drained

2 eggs, lightly beaten

2 tspn Worcestershire sauce

60g (2oz) wholemeal breadcrumbs, made from stale bread

60g (2oz) grated Cheddar cheese

1 Preheat oven to 180°C (350°F/ Gas 4). Cook pasta in boiling salted water following packet directions until *al dente*. Drain well and place in bottom of a greased 2 litre (3¹/2pt) ovenproof dish.

Pasta, Spinach and Tomatoes

2 Place chicken, spring onions, red pepper, pineapple, eggs and Worcestershire sauce in a bowl, mix well and spread evenly over fettucine. Sprinkle with combined breadcrumbs and Cheddar cheese. Bake for 30 minutes or until topping is golden.

Serves 4

Pasta, Spinach and Tomatoes

125ml (4fl oz) olive oil

1 clove garlic, crushed

1/2 small red chilli, halved, seeded and sliced

1/2 tspn salt

freshly ground black pepper

300g (9 1/2 oz) pasta shapes, such as shells, penne, spirals

1 tblspn balsamic vinegar

1 onion, diced

2 tblspn drained capers

155g (5oz) pitted black olives, halved

handful of fresh basil leaves, shredded

500g (1lb) spinach, trimmed, washed and torn into bite-size pieces

315g (10oz) cherry tomatoes, halved

1 red pepper, roasted, skinned and diced

1 Place oil, garlic, red chilli, salt and black pepper to taste in a small bowl, mix well and set aside. Cook pasta in boiling salted water following packet directions until *al dente*. Drain well and place in a large bowl, add oil mixture and vinegar and mix to combine.

2 Add onion, capers, olives, basil, spinach, tomatoes and red pepper to pasta mixture and mix well. Adjust seasonings and serve at room temperature.

Serves 4

Two Pastas with Fresh Vegetables

3 tblspn olive oil

2 cloves garlic, chopped

440g (14oz) chopped canned tomatoes in juice, undrained

8-10 fresh basil leaves or oregano sprigs, chopped

freshly ground black pepper

1/2 small head broccoli, cut into florets

8 spears asparagus, trimmed and sliced

8 mangetout, strings removed

2 small courgettes, cut into sticks

500g (1lb) spiral, bow or shell pasta

500g (1lb) tagliatelle, or other ribbon pasta

extra fresh basil leaves

125g (4oz) freshly grated Parmesan cheese

1 Heat oil in a small saucepan over moderate heat, add garlic and cook until golden. Add tomatoes and their juice and bring to the boil. Reduce heat and simmer, stirring occasionally, for 5 minutes. Add basil or oregano and season to taste with black pepper.

2 Boil, steam or microwave vegetables until just tender. Drain and add to tomato sauce.

3 Cook pastas separately in boiling salted water following packet directions until *al dente*. Drain and place in a large bowl. Add vegetable mixture and toss to combine. Serve in heated bowls topped with extra basil and Parmesan cheese.

Serves 6

Pasta with Mushroom Sauce

125ml (4fl oz) olive oil

1 large onion, finely chopped

1 clove garlic, finely chopped

500g (1lb) small button mushrooms, thinly sliced

freshly ground black pepper

90ml (3fl oz) dry white wine

3-4 canned anchovy fillets, drained and chopped

3 large ripe tomatoes, peeled and diced

3 tblspn chopped fresh parsley

315g (10oz) spaghetti or vermicelli

1 Heat half the oil in a frying pan over moderate heat, add onion and garlic and cook, stirring, until onion is transparent. Add mushrooms and season to taste with black pepper. Cook, stirring frequently, for 5 minutes or until mushrooms are cooked and all liquid evaporates.

2 Add wine to pan and bring to the boil. Briskly simmer a few minutes, then stir in achovies, tomatoes and parsley. Reduce heat, cover and gently simmer for 15 minutes or until sauce thickens.

3 Cook pasta in boiling salted water following packet directions until *al dente*. Drain well and return to pan, add mushroom sauce and toss well to combine. Drizzle with remaining oil and serve immediately.

Serves 4

Noodles Polonaise

250g (8oz) wide ribbon pasta

60g (2oz) butter

60g (2oz) breadcrumbs, made from stale bread

2 hard-boiled eggs, chopped

1 tblspn snipped fresh chives

1/2 tspn salt

1 Cook pasta in boiling salted water following packet directions until *al dente*. Drain and rinse in hot water and drain again.

2 Melt butter in a frying pan over moderate heat, add breadcrumbs and cook until golden brown. Add eggs, chives and salt to mixture and briefly stir over heat to combine. Spoon mixture over pasta on heated serving plates and serve immediately.

Serves 4-6

Penne, Peppers and Courgettes

30g (1oz) butter

1 yellow or red pepper, roasted, skinned and diced

2 courgettes, diced

3 tomatoes, peeled, seeded and diced

3 spring onions, sliced

280g (9oz) penne

1 tblspn chopped fresh parsley

freshly ground black pepper

1 Melt butter in a large frying pan over moderate heat, add yellow or red pepper and cook, stirring, for 5 minutes. Add courgettes, tomatoes and spring onions and cook for 5 minutes or until vegetables are just tender.

2 Cook penne in boiling salted water following packet directions until *al dente*. Drain well and return to pan, add vegetable mixture and toss to combine. Sprinkle servings with parsley and black pepper to taste.

Serves 4

Pasta 'alla Matriciana'

Macaroni Cream

280g (9oz) macaroni of your choice

3 egg yolks at room temperature

6 tblspn freshly grated Parmesan cheese

125g (4oz) cream cheese or neufchatel cheese, chopped

freshly ground black pepper

freshly grated nutmeg

1 Cook macaroni in boiling salted water following packet directions until *al dente*. Drain well.

2 Place egg yolks and Parmesan cheese in a large deep heatproof bowl and mix to combine. Place bowl over a saucepan of simmering water so that it is heated by the steam. Add cream cheese or neufchatel, black pepper and nutmeg to taste and mix to combine. Add very hot macaroni, toss well to coat and serve immediately.

Serves 4

Pasta with Garlic and Herbs

250g (8oz) pasta of your choice

2 tblspn olive oil

3 cloves garlic, sliced

60g (2oz) butter

6-8 tblspn chopped mixed fresh herbs

1/2 tspn salt

freshly ground black pepper

170ml (5 1/2 fl oz) milk

1 Cook pasta in boiling salted water following packet directions until *al dente*. Drain well.

2 Heat oil in a large frying pan over moderate heat, add garlic and cook until golden. Take care not to burn garlic or it will be bitter.

3 Add hot pasta and butter to pan and toss to coat. Add herbs, salt and black pepper to taste and toss again. Gradually add milk to pan and cook, stirring, until milk absorbs and forms a sauce. Serve immediately.

Serves 4

Pasta 'alla Matriciana'

3 tblspn olive oil

1 onion, thinly sliced

155g (5oz) lean bacon or pancetta, diced

125ml (4fl oz) dry white wine

500g (1lb) tomatoes, peeled, seeded and chopped or 440g (14oz) chopped canned tomatoes in juice, undrained

1 small dried chilli, optional

freshly ground black pepper

500g (1lb) dried pasta or 250g (8oz) fresh pasta of your choice

90g (3oz) freshly grated Parmesan cheese

1 Heat oil in a saucepan over moderate heat, add onion and cook until tender. Add bacon or pancetta and cook for 2-3 minutes.

Add wine to pan and bring to the boil, reduce heat and simmer until liquid reduces slightly.

2 Add tomatoes and chilli (if using) to mixture and season to taste with black pepper. Bring to the boil, reduce heat and simmer for 15 minutes. Remove chilli.

3 Cook pasta in boiling salted water, 6-8 minutes for dried pasta, 3-4 minutes for fresh pasta, or until *al dente*. Drain well and return to pan. Add sauce to pasta, toss to combine and serve with Parmesan cheese.

Kitchen Tip
A fiery hot tomato sauce with bacon. Italians like it best with bucatini – tubular strands of pasta. Spaghetti is good too.

Linguine with Spinach and Garlic

300g (9¹/₂oz) linguine or spaghetti

2 tblspn olive oil

3 cloves garlic, thinly sliced

2-3 slices fresh seeded red chilli

500g (1lb) spinach or rocket washed, trimmed and roughly chopped

250ml (8fl oz) chicken stock

freshly grated Parmesan cheese

1 Cook linguine in boiling salted water following packet directions until al dente. Drain well and return to pan.

2 Heat oil in a frying pan over moderate heat, add garlic and red chilli and cook, stirring, until garlic is golden. Add spinach or rocket and stir fry until wilted.

3 Add chicken stock to pan and bring to the boil. Reduce heat and simmer, stirring, for 5 minutes or until spinach or rocket is tender.

4 Add mixture to pasta, toss well and serve immediately drizzled with extra olive oil and sprinkled with Parmesan cheese.

Serves 4

Tortellini Alfredo

500g (1lb) tortellini

125g (4oz) butter

185ml (6fl oz) double cream

4 thin slices ham, cut into strips

125g (4oz) shelled fresh or frozen peas, cooked

90g (3oz) freshly grated Parmesan cheese plus extra to serve

freshly ground black pepper

freshly grated nutmeg

1 Cook tortellini in boiling salted water following packet directions until *al dente*. Drain well.

2 Melt butter in a heavy frying pan over moderate heat, add tortellini and toss to coat. Add cream, ham and peas and cook gently until the cream forms a sauce with the butter and thickens slightly.

3 Stir Parmesan cheese into mixture, season with black pepper and nutmeg to taste. Serve immediately with extra Parmesan cheese and a pepper mill.

Serves 4

Linguine with Spinach and Garlic

Fusilli with Aubergines and Tomatoes

Fusilli with Aubergines and Tomatoes

125ml (4fl oz) olive oil

1 clove garlic

2 aubergines, peeled and cubed

4 tomatoes, peeled, seeded and diced

1-2 tblspn chopped fresh basil

freshly ground black pepper

300g (9¹/₂oz) fusilli

2 tblspn freshly grated Parmesan cheese

1 Heat half the oil in a frying pan over moderate heat, add garlic and aubergines and cook, stirring, until aubergines are golden brown.

2 Add remaining oil to pan, add tomatoes and cook, stirring, for 5 minutes longer. Add basil with black pepper to taste and mix to combine.

3 Cook pasta in boiling salted water following packet directions until *al dente*. Drain well and add to aubergine mixture, tossing to coat. Sprinkle with Parmesan cheese and extra black pepper and serve immediately.

Serves 4

Pasta Shells with Peppers

3 tblspn olive oil

1 onion, thinly sliced

4 red, yellow and/or green peppers, cut into strips

500g (1lb) tomatoes, peeled, seeded and diced

2-3 tblspn chopped fresh basil

freshly ground black pepper

500g (1lb) pasta shells

grated fresh Parmesan cheese to serve

1 Heat oil in a large frying pan over moderately-high heat, add onion and cook, stirring, until golden. Add red, yellow and/or green peppers and cook, stirring, until peppers soften.

2 Add tomatoes, basil and black pepper to taste to mixture and simmer gently, covered, for 15 minutes. Remove lid and continue to cook until the mixture reduces. Adjust seasoning to taste.

3 Cook pasta in boiling salted water following packet directions until *al dente*. Drain well and turn into a warm serving dish. Top with sauce and toss to combine. Sprinkle generously with Parmesan cheese and serve immediately.

Seafood Lasagne

4 tblspn butter

4 tblspn plain flour

500ml (16fl oz) very hot milk

1/4 tspn ground nutmeg

250g (8oz) grated mature Cheddar cheese

no precooking required or instant spinach lasagne sheets

750g (1½lb) boneless white fish fillets, skinned and cut into 2cm (¾in) cubes

2 tblspn chopped fresh parsley

1 Preheat oven to 180°C (350°F/ Gas 4). Melt butter in a large saucepan, stir in flour and cook over moderate heat for 1 minute. Remove pan from heat and gradually stir in milk until well blended. Cook over a moderate heat, stirring constantly, until sauce boils and thickens. Remove from heat, add nutmeg and half the Cheddar cheese and stir until sauce is smooth.

2 Spread one-third of the sauce in bottom of a greased ovenproof dish. Place half the lasagne sheets on top, cover with half the fish and sprinkle with 1 tablespoon parsley.

3 Repeat layers with another third of the sauce, remaining lasagne sheets, fish and parsley. Cover with remaining sauce and sprinkle with remaining Cheddar cheese. Bake for 40 minutes or until top is golden. Set aside to stand for 10-15 minutes before cutting.

Serves 4

Poor Parson's Noodles

250g (8oz) wide ribbon pasta

3 tblspn butter

2 onions, finely chopped

½ green pepper, finely chopped

8-10 button mushrooms, sliced

250g (8oz) minced or finely chopped roast lamb or beef

2 tblspn plain flour

dash Tabasco sauce

pinch fresh or dried thyme or other favourite herb

freshly ground black pepper

500ml (16fl oz) beef stock

1 Cook pasta in boiling salted water following packet directions until *al dente*. Drain, rinse in hot water and drain again.

2 Melt butter in a frying pan over moderate heat, add onions and green pepper and cook, stirring, for 3-4 minutes or until onions are tender. Add mushrooms and cook for 2 minutes longer. Add lamb or beef and heat through, stirring.

3 Add flour to mixture and stir to combine. Add Tabasco sauce, thyme and black pepper to taste. Stir stock into mixture, bring to the boil, reduce heat and simmer, stirring, for 5 minutes. Add noodles to mixture, toss to combine and serve.

Serves 4-6

Seafood Lasagne

Cannelloni

125g (4oz) no precooking required or instant cannelloni tubes

125g (4oz) mozzarella cheese, thinly sliced

Tomato Sauce

60ml (2fl oz) olive oil

1 onion, chopped

1 clove garlic, crushed

440g (14oz) chopped canned tomatoes in juice, crushed

2 tblspn tomato purée

500ml (16fl oz) boiling water

1 tblspn chopped fresh parsley

freshly ground black pepper

Beef and Cheese Filling

500g (1lb) lean minced beef

2 eggs, beaten

2 tblspn olive oil

2 tblspn grated Parmesan cheese

1 tblspn chopped fresh parsley

1 tspn chopped fresh oregano or basil or 1/4 tspn dried oregano or basil

1/2 tspn salt

1 To make sauce, heat oil in a heavy saucepan over moderate heat, add onion and garlic and cook, stirring, until golden brown. Add tomatoes with juice, tomato purée and boiling water and stir to combine. Bring to the boil, reduce heat and simmer for 20 minutes. Add parsley and black pepper to taste. Pour half the sauce into a shallow ovenproof dish.

2 Preheat oven to 180°C (350°F/Gas 4). To make filling, place beef, eggs, oil, Parmesan cheese, parsley, oregano or basil, salt and black pepper to taste in a bowl and mix to combine.

3 Fill cannelloni with filling and arrange over sauce in dish. Cover with remaining sauce and mozzarella cheese. Bake for 45-50 minutes or until golden.

Serves 4-6

Kitchen Tip
If not using instant cannelloni tubes, cook in boiling salted water for 5 minutes only. Drain and rinse in cold water and drain again. Cannelloni should be just flexible enough to handle.

Stuffed Pasta Shells

1 x quantity Light Tomato Sauce, see recipe page 5

375g (12oz) cooked chicken breast fillets or any cooked meat

250g (8oz) button mushrooms

1 egg

2 cloves garlic

2 tblspn chopped fresh parsley

1 tblspn lemon juice

2 tspn dried tarragon

1 tspn freshly ground black pepper

1/2 tspn salt

1/2 tspn Tabasco sauce

20 large pasta shells (conchiglie), 5cm (2in) wide

250g (8oz) grated Gruyère cheese

1 Prepare tomato sauce following recipe directions. Preheat oven to 180°C (350°F/Gas 4).

2 Place chicken, mushrooms, egg, garlic, parsley, lemon juice, tarragon, black pepper, salt and Tabasco sauce in a food processor and process until well combined.

3 Cook pasta shells in boiling salted water following packet directions until *al dente*. Drain. Spoon filling into each shell and place, open-side-up, in a greased ovenproof dish.

4 Sprinkle shells with most of the Gruyère cheese, cover with tomato sauce and remaining cheese. Bake for 30 minutes or until golden brown and bubbling.

Serves 6

Kitchen Tip
If liked, use well seasoned spicy Italian sausage mince to fill the shells and bake as directed above. Cooked cold shells can be filled with seafood salad or herbed chicken salad and served as part of a salad platter garnished with onion rings, black olives, cherry tomatoes and hard-boiled eggs.

Penne with Mushrooms

3 tblspn olive oil

1 clove garlic, chopped

250g (8oz) button mushrooms, sliced

1-2 tblspn chopped fresh parsley

1 tblspn butter

freshly ground black pepper

375g (12oz) penne

4 tblspn freshly grated Parmesan cheese

1 Heat oil in a large saucepan over moderate heat, add garlic and mushrooms and cook, stirring, for 4-5 minutes. Add parsley, butter and black pepper to taste and set aside to keep warm.

2 Cook pasta in boiling salted water following packet directions until *al dente*. Drain. Pour mushroom mixture over pasta and toss to combine. Serve in heated bowls sprinkled with Parmesan cheese and extra parsley, if liked.

Serves 6

Bucatini with Aubergine

1 aubergine, peeled and diced

salt

2 tblspn olive oil

1 onion, finely chopped

2 cloves garlic, finely chopped

4 ripe tomatoes, peeled and chopped

1/2 tspn sugar

freshly ground black pepper

3-4 tblspn chopped fresh parsley

olive or vegetable oil for shallow frying

280g (9oz) bucatini

45g (11/2oz) freshly grated Parmesan cheese

1 Place aubergine in a colander, sprinkle with salt and set aside to drain for 1 hour. Rinse well with cold running water and pat dry with paper towels.

Linguine with Anchovy Sauce

2 Heat oil in a frying pan over moderate heat, add onion and cook, stirring, for 2-3 minutes or until golden. Add garlic to pan and cook for 1 minute longer.

3 Add tomatoes and sugar to pan, season to taste with black pepper and bring to the boil. Reduce heat and simmer for 15 minutes or until liquid reduces. Stir in parsley.

4 Heat 1cm (¹/₂in) oil in a separate frying pan over moderate heat, add aubergine and cook for 3-4 minutes until golden on all sides. Using a slotted spoon, remove aubergine, add to tomato sauce and stir to combine.

5 Cook bucatini in boiling salted water following packet directions until *al dente*. Drain well

and place in a heated serving bowl. Add Parmesan cheese to pasta and toss to coat. Add aubergine sauce and toss again. Serve immediately.

Serves 4

Linguine with Anchovy Sauce

250g (8oz) linguine or spaghetti
90ml (3fl oz) olive oil
2 cloves garlic, crushed
45g (1¹/₂oz) canned anchovy fillets, drained
440g (14oz) chopped canned tomatoes in juice, crushed
60g (2oz) black olives, pitted
3-4 tblspn chopped fresh parsley
freshly ground black pepper

1 Cook pasta in boiling salted water following packet directions until *al dente*. Drain.

2 Heat oil in a heavy-based saucepan over moderate heat, add garlic and anchovies and cook, stirring, for 5 minutes or until anchovies dissolve.

3 Add tomatoes and olives to pan and bring to the boil. Reduce heat and simmer, stirring, for 5 minutes or until thickened. Add parsley and season to taste with black pepper. Add drained, hot pasta to sauce and toss to combine. Serve immediately.

Serves 4

Summertime Pasta

125g (4oz) cauliflower florets

125g (4oz) broccoli florets

250g (8oz) tagliatelle or fettucine

4 tblspn olive oil

2 cloves garlic, crushed

1/4 red pepper, cut into strips

1/4 green pepper, cut into strips

1/2 small narrow aubergine, sliced or cut into strips

2 tblspn chopped fresh basil

1/2 tspn freshly ground black pepper

30g (1oz) freshly grated Parmesan cheese

1 Blanch cauliflower and broccoli in boiling water for 1 minute then plunge into cold water and drain.

2 Cook pasta in boiling salted water following packet directions until *al dente.* Drain.

3 Heat oil in a large frying pan over moderate heat, add garlic and cook, stirring, for 1 minute. Add blanched vegetables, red and green pepper, aubergine and basil and cook, stirring, for 3-4 minutes or until vegetables are just tender.

4 Add pasta to vegetable mixture and toss well to combine. Sprinkle with black pepper and Parmesan cheese and serve immediately.

Serves 4

Macaroni with Four Cheeses

90g (3oz) butter

1 tspn plain flour

250ml (8fl oz) milk

60g (2oz) grated Gruyère cheese

60g (2oz) grated Edam or Gouda cheese

60g (2oz) grated Cheddar cheese

ground white pepper

500g (1lb) macaroni

60g (2oz) freshly grated Parmesan cheese

1 Melt half the butter in a saucepan, stir in flour and cook

over moderate heat for 1 minute. Remove pan from heat and gradually stir in milk until blended. Bring to the boil, reduce heat and simmer, stirring constantly, for 3 minutes longer. Remove pan from the heat and stir in Gruyère, Edam or gouda and Cheddar cheeses. Season to taste with white pepper.

2 Cook macaroni in boiling salted water following packet directions until *al dente.* Drain, place in a deep heated serving dish, add remaining butter and toss to combine. Pour cheese sauce over macaroni, mix lightly, sprinkle with Parmesan cheese and serve immediately.

Serves 4-6

Tortellini with Tomato Sauce

375g (12oz) ripe tomatoes, peeled, seeded and chopped

2-3 fresh oregano sprigs or 6 fresh basil leaves

250ml (8fl oz) double cream

45g (1 1/2oz) butter

freshly ground black pepper

500g (1lb) fresh or frozen tortellini

1 Place tomatoes in a frying pan over moderate heat and cook, stirring, for 10 minutes. Place mixture in a blender or food processor and process until smooth. Return tomato purée to pan, add oregano or basil and simmer gently for 3 minutes.

2 Place cream in a small saucepan over moderate heat, add butter, bring to simmering and gently simmer for 3-5 minutes or until slightly reduced.

3 Remove herb leaves from tomato purée and discard. Stir in cream mixture and season to taste with black pepper.

4 Cook tortellini in boiling salted water following packet directions until *al dente.* Drain well, add to sauce, toss to coat and serve immediately.

Serves 4

Summertime Pasta

ORIENTAL PASTA DISHES

Stir fry combinations and the light, delicate and clear noodle broths beloved of Chinese cooking are featured here as well as some tangy and truly delicious Vietnamese favourites.

Vietnamese Chicken and Noodles

200g (6¹/₂oz) cellophane noodles

750g (1¹/₂lb) boneless chicken breast fillets

1 tblspn olive oil

2 onions, thickly sliced

1 tspn grated fresh ginger

2 tblspn fish sauce

1 tblspn light soy sauce

freshly ground black pepper

125ml (4fl oz) water

fresh coriander sprigs for garnish

Salad

2 tomatoes, sliced

1 onion, sliced

1 cucumber, sliced

sugar, malt vinegar and black pepper

1 Place noodles in a large bowl, cover with boiling water and set aside to stand for 10 minutes then drain. Cut fillets into bite-sized chunks.

2 Heat oil in a large frying pan or wok over moderate heat, add chicken, onions and ginger and stir fry for 3-4 minutes or until chicken is golden. Add fish sauce, soy sauce, black pepper to taste and water and stir to combine. Bring to the boil, reduce heat and simmer for 3 minutes.

3 Add noodles to pan, toss gently and cook for 3 minutes longer or until chicken and noodles are tender. Turn into a serving dish and garnish with coriander. Serve hot with salad.

4 To make salad, arrange tomatoes, onion and cucumber on a serving platter and sprinkle with sugar, vinegar and black pepper to taste.

Serves 6

Chilli Sesame Noodles

500g (1lb) thin linguine or vermicelli

60ml (2fl oz) vegetable oil

8 spring onions, chopped

blanched mixed green vegetables such as asparagus tips, mangetout, peas, broccoli for garnish

Sesame Mayonnaise

1 egg

1 tblspn rice vinegar

2 tblspn light soy sauce

2 tblspn Dijon mustard

3 tblspn sesame oil

375ml (12fl oz) vegetable oil

chilli oil, see Kitchen Tip, page 40

1 To make mayonnaise, place egg in a blender or food processor, add vinegar, soy sauce and mustard and blend for 30 seconds. With motor running, gradually add sesame oil, then vegetable oil and blend until sauce thickens. Add chilli oil to taste and blend well.

2 Cook pasta in boiling salted water following packet directions until *al dente*. Drain well and place in a bowl. Add 60ml (2fl oz) oil, toss to combine and set aside to cool.

3 Add mayonnaise and spring onions to noodles and toss to combine. Turn onto a serving dish, garnish with desired vegetables and serve at room temperature.

Serves 6

Vietnamese Chicken and Noodles

Chilled Oriental Noodles

1 tspn olive oil

1 tblspn peeled and slivered fresh ginger

1/2 tspn sugar

375g (12oz) Chinese egg noodles

1 tblspn sesame oil

375g (12oz) shredded cooked chicken or pork or barbecued pork

3 slices cooked ham, shredded

1 cucumber, peeled and cut into strips

45g (1 1/2oz) bean sprouts

fresh coriander sprigs for garnish

Satay Sauce

2 tblspn sesame seeds, toasted

1 tblspn peanut butter

1 tblspn sesame oil

4 tblspn water

3 tblspn soy sauce

3 tspn vinegar

1-4 tspn chilli oil, or to taste

freshly ground black pepper

1 Place olive oil, ginger and sugar in a cup and set aside to marinate for several hours.

2 Cook noodles in boiling salted water following packet directions until just tender. Drain well, add sesame oil, toss to combine and refrigerate until cold.

3 To make sauce, place sesame seeds in a blender or food processor and blend until crushed. Add peanut butter, sesame oil, water, soy sauce, vinegar, chilli oil and black pepper to taste and blend until combined.

4 Arrange chicken or pork, ham, cucumber and bean sprouts on top of noodles. Add sauce and marinated ginger and toss to combine. Garnish with coriander and serve.

Serves 4-6

Kitchen Tip

Chilli oil can be made by heating 2 tablespoons oil in a small frying pan and frying 2 chopped red chillies until they turn dark. Strain the oil and store in a small jar. Alternatively, substitute with Tabasco sauce to taste.

Chicken Noodle Soup

60g (2oz) cellophane noodles

4 Chinese dried mushrooms

1.5 litres (2 1/2pt) chicken stock

4 boneless chicken breast fillets

1 tblspn vegetable oil

1 onion, halved and cut into slivers

2 tspn fish sauce

1/4 tspn ground white pepper

4 spring onions, shredded diagonally

6 fresh coriander sprigs

1 Soak noodles and mushrooms separately in cold water to cover for 30 minutes and drain. Cut noodles into 5cm (2in) lengths. Cut off and discard stems from mushrooms and slice caps into strips.

2 Place stock in a large saucepan and bring to the boil. Add chicken breasts, reduce heat and gently poach for 5-6 minutes or until cooked. Remove pan from heat, remove chicken from stock and set aside until cool enough to handle. Shred chicken into strips about 4cm (1 1/4in) long and 1cm (1/2in) wide.

3 Heat oil in a frying pan or wok over moderate heat, add onion and stir fry for 1-2 minutes or until golden. Add chicken and mushrooms to pan and stir fry for 1 minute more.

4 Bring stock to simmering, add chicken mixture with fish sauce, white pepper and noodles and simmer for 5 minutes. Just before serving, sprinkle soup with spring onions and coriander.

Serves 6

Noodle and Prawn Salad

250g (8oz) rice vermicelli

500g (1lb) cooked, peeled and deveined prawns

125g (4oz) fresh bean sprouts

90g (3oz) shredded lettuce

8 spring onions, chopped

1 bunch fresh mint leaves

1 bunch fresh coriander leaves

155g (5oz) roasted unsalted peanuts, roughly chopped

3 tblspn shredded, seeded, hot green chillies

Nuoc Cham Sauce

2 cloves garlic, peeled

4 dried red chillies or 1 fresh red chilli, chopped

6 tspn sugar

juice and pulp of 1 lime

8 tblspn fish sauce

90ml (3fl oz) water

1 To make sauce, place garlic, chillies and sugar in a blender or food processor and blend to a paste. With motor runnng, add lime juice and pulp, then fish sauce, blending until smooth. Add water and blend to combine. Store in a covered glass container.

2 Cook noodles in boiling water for 2-3 minutes or until tender. Drain well and transfer to a serving platter. Scatter with prawns, sprouts, lettuce, spring onions, herbs, peanuts and green chillies. Sprinkle sauce over salad, toss lightly and serve.

Serves 4-6

Chow Mein

250g (8oz) Chinese egg noodles

6 tblspn vegetable oil

2 boneless chicken breast fillets, shredded or 375g (12oz) peeled and deveined uncooked prawns, halved lengthwise

125ml (4fl oz) Chinese rice wine or dry sherry

3 tblspn soy sauce

2 tblspn sugar

1 tspn salt

1/2 tspn grated fresh ginger

vinegar to serve

1 Cook noodles in boiling water following packet directions. Drain and rinse under cold water and drain again. Spread noodles out thinly on a damp tea-towel and place in a cool airy place to dry.

2 Heat 2 tablespoons oil in a wok or frying pan over moderate heat, add chicken or prawns and stir fry until just half cooked. Add half each of the wine or sherry, soy sauce and sugar and cook for 2 minutes longer or until chicken or prawns are tender. Remove from pan and set aside to keep warm.

3 Heat remaining oil in pan, add noodles and cook, turning from time to time with a fork, until golden brown. Add remaining wine or sherry, soy sauce, sugar, salt and ginger and cook briskly for 2 minutes longer. Return chicken or prawns to pan, heat through, sprinkle with vinegar to taste and serve immediately.

Serves 4

Beef with Cellophane Noodles

375g (12oz) lean beef steak, cut into thin strips

1 egg white

1 tspn cornflour

1 tspn salt

2 tblspn groundnut (peanut) oil

1 leek, thinly sliced

1 tblspn soy sauce

1/4 tspn chilli oil, see Kitchen Tip page 40

250ml (8fl oz) groundnut (peanut) oil, extra

30g (1oz) cellophane noodles, soaked in hot water for 10 minutes.

1 Place beef in a bowl, add egg white, cornflour and 1/2 teaspoon salt and mix well to combine. Set aside to stand for 5 minutes.

2 Heat 2 tablespoons oil in a wok or frying pan over moderate heat, add beef mixture and stir fry for 2 minutes. Add leek and stir fry for 1 minute longer. Add soy sauce and chilli oil and mix well to combine. Set aside to keep warm.

3 Drain noodles well. Heat 250ml (8fl oz) oil in a deep frying pan over moderate heat until a cube of bread browns in 50 seconds and deep-fry noodles for 1-2 seconds. Take care to avoid burning. Remove with a slotted spoon and set aside to drain on paper towels. Sprinkle noodles with remaining salt, place on a serving platter, top with beef mixture and serve.

Serves 4

Sesame Chicken with Rice Noodles

750g (1 1/2 lb) chicken thigh joints and breast fillets, skin removed

250g (8oz) Chinese rice noodles

1 tblspn sesame oil

2 tblspn vegetable oil

1 tblspn shredded fresh ginger

125ml (4fl oz) Chinese rice wine or dry sherry

750ml (1 1/4 pt) chicken stock

1 tspn sugar

1 tspn salt

6 leaves spinach, chopped

1 With a cleaver or heavy knife, chop chicken through bones into bite-sized pieces. Soak noodles in warm water to cover for 5 minutes. Drain well.

2 Heat sesame and vegetable oils in a wok or frying pan over moderate heat until hot. Add ginger and stir fry for 30 seconds. Add chicken pieces and stir fry for 3-5 minutes until golden.

3 Add wine or sherry to pan, bring to the boil and add stock, sugar and salt. Reduce heat and simmer for 15 minutes or until chicken is tender.

4 Stir noodles into pan and cook for 5 minutes longer. Add spinach just before serving and cook until wilted. Ladle into heated bowls.

Serves 4

Shredded Lamb with Bamboo Shoots

1 tblspn olive oil

4 lean lamb leg chops

4-6 spring onions, chopped

2 cloves garlic, crushed

250ml (8fl oz) beef stock

60ml (2fl oz) white wine

1 tblspn soy sauce

1 tspn Chinese five spice powder

1 tspn chilli paste (sambal oelek)

2 tspn olive oil, extra

2-3 spring onions, chopped, extra

125g (4oz) bamboo shoots

250g (8oz) rice vermicelli

1 Heat oil in a large frying pan over moderate heat. Add lamb chops and seer on both sides, then transfer to a large saucepan. Add spring onions and garlic to frying pan, cook for 2 minutes and add to lamb.

2 Add stock, wine, soy sauce, five spice powder and sambal oelek (chilli paste) to lamb and bring to the boil. Reduce heat, cover and gently simmer for 1 hour. With a slotted spoon remove lamb from pan and set aside to cool. Cut lamb into shreds. Strain stock through sieve and reserve.

3 Heat extra oil in frying pan over moderate heat, add remaining spring onions and stir fry for 2 minutes. Add shredded lamb and

Shredded Lamb with Bamboo Shoots

bamboo shoots and stir fry for 1 minute longer. Add reserved stock to pan and heat through.

4 Cook noodles in boiling water following packet directions until tender, about 1 minute. Drain well and serve in heated bowls topped with lamb mixture.

Serves 4

Beef, Peppers and Fried Noodles

250g (8oz) thin egg noodles

250g (8oz) lean beef steak, cut into thin strips

4 tblspn dark soy sauce

1 tblspn Chinese rice wine or dry sherry

freshly ground black pepper

2 tspn sugar

2 tspn cornflour

8-9 tblspn water

4 tblspn vegetable oil

1 onion, cut into six and divided into petals

1 green pepper, cubed

2 cloves garlic, crushed

4 slices peeled fresh ginger

1 Cook noodles in boiling salted water for 2 minutes. Drain and rinse under cold water and drain again. Spread noodles out thinly on a damp tea-towel and place in a cool airy place to dry.

2 Place beef in a bowl with 2 tablespoons soy sauce, wine, black pepper, and 1 teaspoon each sugar and cornflour. Mix well to combine and set aside to marinate.

3 Place remaining soy sauce, sugar and cornflour in a separate bowl with enough water to make a thin sauce.

4 Heat 1 tablespoon oil in a frying pan or wok over moderate heat, add half the noodles and stir fry until golden. Transfer to a heated serving plate and set aside to keep warm. Repeat with another tablespoon oil and remaining noodles.

5 Heat remaining oil in same pan over moderate heat, add onion and green pepper and stir fry for 2 minutes. Add garlic, ginger and beef mixture and stir fry for 1 minute longer. Add cornflour mixture to pan and bring to the boil, stirring. Serve beef mixture over noodles.

Serves 4

Braised Pork with Noodles

375g (12oz) lean pork fillet, in one piece

2 tblspn soy sauce

2 tblspn Chinese rice wine or sherry

1 tblspn chopped spring onion

1 tspn grated fresh ginger

freshly ground black pepper

1 tblspn groundnut (peanut) oil

1 tspn sugar

500ml (16fl oz) chicken stock

250g (8oz) Chinese egg noodles, cooked and kept warm

1 Place pork in a bowl, add 1 tablespoon soy sauce, 1 tablespoon rice wine or sherry, spring onion, ginger and black pepper. Mix well and set aside to marinate for 20 minutes. Drain meat and reserve marinade.

2 Heat oil in a frying pan over moderate heat, add pork and cook until brown on all sides. Add sugar and reserved marinade and bring to the boil. Reduce heat and simmer until all liquid evaporates. Remove pork from pan and slice.

3 Place stock in a saucepan over a moderate heat, add remaining soy sauce and wine or sherry and bring to the boil. Place noodles in serving bowls, add stock and top with pork. Serve hot.

Serves 4-6

Hot and Sour Soup

125g (4oz) lean pork fillet, thinly shredded

2 tblspn light soy sauce

2 tspn cornflour

freshly ground black pepper

1 tblspn vegetable oil

1-1.2 litres (1³/4-2pt) chicken stock

60g (2oz) thinly shredded bamboo shoots

5 Chinese dried mushrooms, soaked and shredded

250g (8oz) bean curd, slivered

45g (1¹/₂oz) vermicelli, soaked until softened

2 tblspn vinegar

3 eggs, beaten until foamy

2 tblspn cornflour blended with 125ml (4fl oz) cold water

fresh coriander for garnish

1 Place pork, soy sauce, 2 teaspoons cornflour and black pepper to taste in a bowl, toss well to combine.

2 Heat oil in a saucepan over a moderate heat, add pork mixture and cook, stirring, for 15 seconds. Add stock, bamboo shoots, mushrooms, bean curd and vermicelli and bring to the boil. Reduce heat and simmer for 10 minutes.

3 Stir vinegar into mixture, season to taste with black pepper, then whisk in eggs. Add blended cornflour to soup and simmer until thickened. Serve garnished with coriander.

Serves 6

Fragrant Noodles

20 Chinese dried prawns

8 Chinese dried mushrooms

125ml (4fl oz) groundnut (peanut) oil

3 onions, chopped

1 tblspn light soy sauce

2 tspn Chinese rice wine or dry sherry

500ml (16fl oz) water

500g (1lb) Chinese egg noodles

1 Soak prawns and mushrooms separately in cold water for 10 minutes, then drain. Clean prawns and remove mushroom stems and halve or slice caps.

2 Heat half the oil in a wok or frying pan over moderate heat, add onions and stir fry for 2-3 minutes. Reduce heat slightly, add prawns and mushrooms and stir fry until liquid evaporates. Remove pan from heat.

3 Heat remaining oil in a saucepan, add prawn mixture, soy sauce and wine or sherry and stir-fry for 1-2 minutes. Add water, bring to the boil, reduce heat and simmer for 20 minutes or until water has nearly evaporated.

4 Meanwhile, cook noodles in boiling water following packet directions until tender, drain, rinse under cold water and drain again. Add noodles to pan, toss to combine and serve.

Serves 4

Nutty Vegetables and Noodles

375g (12oz) egg noodles

vegetable oil for deep-frying

500ml (16fl oz) chicken stock

1 red pepper, cut into strips

125g (4oz) mangetout, strings removed, cut into strips

125g (4oz) bean sprouts

440g (14oz) canned baby sweet corn

1 tblspn cornflour

2 tblspn Chinese rice wine or dry sherry

60g (2oz) peanut butter

1 tblspn light soy sauce

1 tspn sesame oil

1 Cook noodles in boiling water following packet directions until just tender. Drain and spread out thinly on a tea-towel and set aside to completely dry.

2 Heat vegetable oil in a large saucepan until a cube of bread dropped in browns in 50 seconds. Lower noodles into hot oil and cook until puffed and golden. Remove noodles with a slotted spoon and drain on paper towels.

3 Bring stock to the boil in a wok or frying pan, add red pepper, mangetout, bean sprouts and corn, cover and cook until mangetout are just tender.

Nutty Vegetables and Noodles

4 Place cornflour, wine or sherry, peanut butter, soy sauce and sesame oil in a bowl, stir to combine, then stir into vegetable mixture. Add noodles and cook, stirring, until mixture boils and thickens. Serve immediately.

Serves 4

Chicken and Noodle Stir Fry

375g (12oz) wide Chinese egg noodles

1 tblspn soy sauce

1 tblspn Chinese rice wine or dry sherry

4 boneless chicken breast fillets, sliced lengthwise into strips

1 tblspn cornflour

2 tblspn cold water

1 tblspn oyster sauce

1/2 tspn salt

2 tblspn groundnut (peanut) oil

2 cloves garlic, crushed

1 tspn grated fresh ginger

1/2 Chinese cabbage, leaves separated and cut into bite-sized pieces

250ml (8fl oz) chicken stock

4-5 spring onions, chopped for garnish

1 Cook noodles in boiling water following packet directions until tender. Drain well, rinse and drain again.

2 Place soy sauce and wine or sherry in a bowl, add chicken, toss to coat and set aside to marinate. Place cornflour in a small bowl, add cold water, oyster sauce and salt and mix well.

3 Heat oil in a wok or frying pan over moderate heat, add garlic and ginger and stir fry for 2-3 minutes or until golden. Add chicken mixture and stir fry for 2-3 minutes or until golden brown. Add cabbage and stir fry for 1 minute longer.

4 Add stock to pan, bring to simmering, stir in cornflour mixture and simmer, stirring, until mixture thickens. Add drained noodles to pan, toss to combine and serve garnished with spring onions.

Serves 4-6

Singapore Noodles

250g (8oz) rice vermicelli

6 tblspn vegetable oil

250g (8oz) peeled and deveined prawns, cut into 1cm (1/2in) pieces

1 small onion, chopped

1/2 red pepper, cut into thin strips

60g (2oz) bean sprouts

1 tspn hot curry powder or curry paste

1 egg, lightly beaten

185g (6oz) shredded barbecued or roast pork, optional

freshly ground black pepper

1 tblspn sesame oil

2 tblspn roughly chopped fresh coriander leaves

1 Cook noodles in boiling salted water following packet directions for 2-3 minutes or until tender. Drain, rinse and drain again. Spread noodles out on a tea-towel and set aside to completely dry.

2 Heat 1 tablespoon oil in a wok or large frying pan until hot but not smoking. Add prawns and stir-fry for 1 minute or until they change colour. Remove prawns and set aside to keep warm.

3 Heat 2 tablespoons oil in the same wok over moderate heat, add onion and red pepper and stir fry for 1 minute. Add bean sprouts and stir fry for 1 minute longer. Remove mixture and set aside with prawns.

4 Add remaining oil to wok over moderate heat, add curry powder or paste, noodles and egg and stir fry until thoroughly combined.

5 Return prawn mixture to wok, add pork (if using) and toss well to combine. Season to taste with black pepper and stir fry for 8 minutes longer. Transfer to a serving platter, drizzle with sesame oil and sprinkle with coriander.

Serves 4-6

Fried Hokkien Noodles

500g (1lb) fresh yellow hokkien noodles

3 tblspn vegetable oil

250g (8oz) small uncooked prawns, peeled and deveined, heads and shells reserved

250ml (8fl oz) fish stock or water

6-8 large cloves garlic, crushed

2 eggs, lightly beaten

250g (8oz) bean sprouts

250g (8oz) barbecued or roast pork or cooked chicken, thinly sliced

freshly ground black pepper

For garnish:

fresh red chillies, thinly sliced

4 spring onions, cut into 2.5cm (1in) lengths

2-3 stalks celery, finely chopped

1 Soak noodles in enough boiling water to cover for 5-8 minutes or until tender, drain and set aside.

2 Heat 1 tablespoon oil in a wok or large frying pan over moderate heat, add prawn heads and shells and stir fry for 2 minutes. Add fish stock or water, bring to the boil, reduce heat and simmer for 5 minutes. Strain stock and return to pan. Discard shells. Bring stock to the boil, reduce heat, add prawns and poach until cooked. Strain and reserve stock and set prawns aside.

3 Heat remaining oil in a clean wok over moderate heat, add garlic and stir fry for 1-2 minutes or until fragrant. Increase heat, add eggs and cook, stirring constantly, for 1 minute. Add noodles, bean sprouts and 125ml (4fl oz) reserved stock.

4 Add prawns and pork or chicken to mixture, season to taste with black pepper, toss well to combine and stir fry for 2-3 minutes longer. Serve garnished with chillies, spring onions and celery.

Serves 4-6

Kitchen Tip
Look for fresh hokkien noodles at Oriental food stores, but if unavailable, substitute with Italian bucatini – the hollow spaghetti.

Vermicelli and Pork with Bean Sauce

2-3 Chinese dried mushrooms

125g (4oz) rice vermicelli

1 tblspn Chinese rice wine or dry sherry

1 tblspn soy sauce

1/2 tspn salt

250ml (8fl oz) chicken stock

5 tblspn vegetable oil

125g (4oz) lean minced pork

3 tblspn finely chopped spring onions

2-3 fresh or dried red chillies, finely chopped

1 tblspn chopped fresh ginger

1-2 tblspn hot bean sauce

1/2 green pepper, shredded

1 Soak mushrooms in enough hot water to cover until softened, drain, discard stems and slice caps. Soak vermicelli in hot water for 5 minutes or until transparent and soft. Drain well, cut lengths into thirds and toss with a few drops of oil. Place wine or sherry, soy sauce, salt and stock in a bowl and set aside.

2 Heat 4 tablespoons oil in a wok or large frying pan over moderate heat, add pork and stir fry for 2-3 minutes or until cooked. Add spring onions, chillies, ginger, bean sauce and mushrooms to pan and stir fry for 3-4 minutes.

3 Add stock mixture and vermicelli to pan, bring to the boil, reduce heat and simmer, stirring occasionally, until all liquid evaporates. Turn into a serving bowl. Quickly fry green pepper in remaining oil and sprinkle over the top.

Serves 4

Index

Managing Editor: Rachel Blackmore
Editors: Kirsten John, Linda Venturoni
Production Manager: Sheridan Carter
Senior Production Editor: Anna Maguire
Production Editor: Sheridan Packer
Picture Editor: Kirsten Holmes
Editorial and Production Assistant: Danielle Thiris
Layout and Finished Art: Stephen Joseph
Cover Styling: Janet Mitchell

Published by J.B. Fairfax Press Pty Limited
80-82 McLachlan Avenue
Rushcutters Bay, NSW 2011
A.C.N. 003 738 430

Formatted by J.B.Fairfax Press Pty Limited
Printed by Toppan Printing Co, Singapore
PRINTED IN SINGAPORE

JBFP 381 A/UK
Includes Index
ISBN 1 86343 116 0 (set)
ISBN 1 86343 214 0

Distribution and Sales Enquiries
Australia: J.B. Fairfax Press Pty Limited
Ph: (02) 361 6366 Fax: (02) 360 6262
United Kingdom: J.B. Fairfax Press Limited
Ph (0933) 402330 Fax: (0933) 402234